Who Is
Willie Nelson?

by David Stabler

illustrated by Tim Foley

Penguin Workshop

For Buggs and Vickie—TF

PENGUIN WORKSHOP
An imprint of Penguin Random House LLC
1745 Broadway, New York, New York 10019

First published in the United States of America by Penguin Workshop,
an imprint of Penguin Random House LLC, 2025

Visit us online at penguinrandomhouse.com.

Library of Congress Cataloging-in-Publication Data is available.

Printed in the United States of America

ISBN 9780593886533 (paperback)   10 9 8 7 6 5 4 3 2 1 CJKW
ISBN 9780593886540 (library binding)   10 9 8 7 6 5 4 3 2 1 CJKW

The authorized representative in the EU for product safety and compliance is
Penguin Random House Ireland, Morrison Chambers, 32 Nassau Street,
Dublin D02 YH68, Ireland, https://eu-contact.penguin.ie.

Contents

Who Is Willie Nelson?

One day in 1938, in a little town called Abbott, Texas, a five-year-old redheaded boy named Willie Nelson stepped in front of a crowd at the town's church picnic. He wore a fancy white sailor suit and held a poem given to him by his grandmother.

Little Willie had always liked to perform, and people's eyes seemed to be on him wherever he went. This time, however, his audience was much larger than just a few people. It seemed like every family in town had gathered for the big party. Neighbors prayed, sang songs, ate food, and chatted with each other.

The stage for Willie's performance was just the back of a big truck. But to a five-year-old, that seemed like an impossibly high mountain. Willie

was nervous as he climbed up to the stage. So nervous, in fact, that he did what many little kids do when they're nervous—he picked his nose! So much so, that it started to bleed.

By the time it was Willie's turn to speak to the crowd, his white sailor suit had little red spots on it from his bloody nose. But Willie didn't let that stop him. Taking a deep breath, he stood up there and started to recite. But instead of reciting the poem from his grandma, he made up his own.

As he spoke, he held one nostril shut with his

hand to stop his nosebleed. In a pinched but clear voice, Willie said:

What are you looking at me for?
I ain't got nothin' to say.
If you don't like the looks of me
You can look some other way.

As the crowd clapped and cheered, Willie was

happy and relieved. He had not stumbled over his words, and it seemed as if everyone at the picnic really liked him. He enjoyed being the center of attention, making everyone smile. The people in the audience felt like his family, and he gave them a big, thankful grin. When he stepped down, he knew he wanted to keep putting on shows.

From that day on, everyone in Abbott called Willie Nelson "Booger Red" because of his nosebleed. But they weren't making fun of him. They were encouraging him. They wanted to hear more from Willie. And over the years, they would. This is the story of how that shy Central Texas farm boy grew into one of the world's most beloved entertainers.

CHAPTER 1
Texas Childhood

Willie Hugh Nelson was born in the town of Abbott in Hill County in Central Texas on April 29, 1933. His parents were Myrle Marie and Ira Doyle Nelson.

Ira and Myrle Nelson

His cousin Mildred gave him the name Willie. She also chose Hugh as his middle name to remember her brother who had passed away.

Willie's family had a long history in America, going all the way back to the time of the American Revolution. One of his ancestors, John Nelson, was even a major in the war for independence. Willie's parents came to Texas from Arkansas in 1929 to find jobs during the Great Depression.

Willie had a sister named Bobbie who was two years older than he was. Sadly, Willie's mom left the family not long after he was born, and his dad got married again and moved away. Willie and Bobbie were left to be raised by their grandparents, whom they called Mama and Daddy Nelson. Daddy Nelson was a blacksmith. Both he and Mama also worked as music teachers.

The Great Depression

The Great Depression started when the stock market crashed in 1929, which meant that people lost a lot of the money that they had invested. This forced many businesses to close, and many people to lose their jobs. It was a very sad time in American history.

People didn't have enough money to pay for things they needed, like their homes, food, and clothes. Families had to stand in long lines just to get some food to eat. The economic hardships lasted all through the 1930s. They did not truly end until the United States entered World War II in 1941.

Willie was a playful toddler who was sometimes
difficult to control. Sometimes Mama Nelson
had to tie him to a pole to keep him from
wandering off. School was just "okay" for Willie.
He liked listening to music more than paying
attention in class.

Willie's sister, Bobbie, was always a better student than he was. From an early age, Bobbie learned to read music and play the piano. By the time she was ten, she was known all across the county as a piano prodigy—a person with exceptional talent.

Willie took an interest in a different instrument. When he was six years old, his grandparents bought him his first guitar. Daddy Nelson even taught him how to play it.

Willie loved performing right from the start. On Sundays, he and Bobbie sang songs in the town church together. Hymns like "Amazing

Grace" and "Rock of Ages" were a source of joy for Willie, even if he didn't always know what the words meant. Before long, Willie started trying to come up with his own lyrics. He wrote his first song when he was just seven years old.

Besides music, Willie also liked going to the movies. Westerns were his favorite type of movie. Willie enjoyed watching the cowboy heroes ride across the range. Sometimes they even carried their guitars with them and sang. Songs like "Happy Trails to You" and "Back in the Saddle Again" weren't like the hymns Willie learned in church, but they inspired him in the same kind of way. "Singing cowboys" like Tex Ritter, Gene Autry, and Roy Rogers became people that Willie looked up to and wanted to imitate.

Willie also enjoyed reading comic books and learning about martial arts. He taught himself jujitsu and judo by reading instructional pamphlets. He raised calves and hogs and helped with the gardening on the family farm. But because times were so tough during the Depression, his family often had difficulty paying for groceries.

Singing Cowboys

"Singing cowboys" got their start in the 1930s, around the time when radio became popular and silent movies gave way to "talkies." They were performers who sang and rode horses. Gene Autry and Roy Rogers were two of the most famous singing cowboys of this era. They appeared as cowboys in movies and also sang on the radio.

Gene Autry and Roy Rogers

Their songs were mostly about being brave, finding love, and going on adventures. Singing cowboys were most popular during difficult times like the Great Depression and World War II, when people looked up to them as heroes. By the 1950s, when movie westerns started to decline, the era of the singing cowboy had come to an end.

During the summer when he wasn't in school, Willie and his family had to pick cotton in the fields to earn extra money. But Willie didn't like picking cotton. It was difficult, backbreaking work, especially in the scorching hot Texas summers. Sometimes Willie and his friends would uncover bumblebee nests while working in the fields. They went home and made paddles out of old wooden apple crates. Then they returned to the fields to battle the bumblebees with their paddles. Willie got stung a lot, and his eyes would swell up because of the stings.

Willie wanted to find a safer way to earn money. One day he walked into the town barbershop with his guitar and started singing. One of the customers handed Willie a quarter.

That was the first time he earned money from his music. Later, Willie put together a hand-drawn book of fifteen of his own songs, entitled "Songs by Willie Nelson." But nobody wanted to buy his songs just yet.

Willie had decided that someway, somehow, he would make a living off his musical talents. But how?

CHAPTER 2
Honky-Tonk Nights

Once Willie earned that quarter in the barbershop, he knew that playing music was what he wanted to do for the rest of his life. People in Abbott also began to notice Willie's talent. Even though he couldn't read music like his sister, Bobbie, they could tell that he was really good at playing music by ear. (That means by hearing it, not by reading the notes.) Soon local bands began asking Willie if he wanted to play with them.

When he was just nine years old, Willie was lucky enough to get a job playing guitar in a band called Bohemian Polka. Bohemian Polka played in dance halls, taverns, and musical bars known as "honky-tonks."

Willie's new job didn't go over all that well with Mama Nelson. She didn't like the idea of a young boy staying up late and being around so much dancing and drinking. Then she found out how much money Willie was making: eight dollars a night. That was as much as he made working in the fields for an entire week! It was a lot of money in 1942. "I never did get her approval," Willie later said, "but I also didn't get any flak."

He continued playing with Bohemian Polka for the next few years.

Over time, Willie got tired of playing polka, which is a traditional style of dance music from Eastern Europe. The music's oompah-pah rhythms were not really Willie's style. Besides, no one ever played polka on the radio, which was the way most people learned about music in those days.

Since many people couldn't afford record players, and television had only recently been invented, families gathered around the radio to hear the latest news and entertainment.

The more Willie listened to the radio, the more he liked the music of country-and-western musicians like Hank Williams, Bob Wills, Lefty Frizzell, and Ernest Tubb. Listening to them made him want to play his own music in their style.

When he was fourteen, Willie started going to Abbott High School. There he kept up his music studies and also played sports like football, basketball, and baseball. Around this time, Willie's sister, Bobbie, married a man named Bud Fletcher. Bud and Bobbie started up their own country-and-western band called Bud Fletcher and the Texans. Bobbie played piano. Bud couldn't play an instrument, so instead, he stuck a broom handle into a bucket of sand and slapped it like a stand-up bass. They asked Willie to join the group and play guitar.

Bud Fletcher and the Texans played music in bars and honky-tonks all across Central Texas. They also had their own weekly radio show on station KHBR in Hillsboro, Texas. Before long, Willie became the most popular member of the group. He even had his own fan club, made up of teenage girls who gave him a fancy suit to wear onstage.

Hank Williams (1923–1953)

Hiram "Hank" Williams was a famous twentieth-century singer and songwriter who was known as the "Hillbilly Shakespeare." He was born in Mount Olive, Alabama, and started singing on the radio when he was a  teenager. In 1947, when he was just twenty-four, he had his first big hit with a song he wrote called "Move It on Over." Some of his other well-known songs are "I'm So Lonesome I Could Cry," "Your Cheatin' Heart," and "Hey, Good Lookin'." Sadly, Williams died when he was only twenty-nine years old.

Even though his career was very short, Hank Williams had a huge influence on other musicians. He is remembered as country music's first superstar and one of the greatest country singers of all time.

Willie spent three years playing with the band. But when he graduated from high school in 1950, he didn't know what to do next. He tried to get a college baseball scholarship, but didn't make it. He worked for a short time as a telephone operator, then got a job working in a pawn shop (a store that lends money in exchange for a person's valuable items) in Abbott. But that didn't work out, either. Eventually, he moved to the nearby town of Tyler, Texas, and took a job cutting down trees for the company that kept the electrical power lines clear. But that turned out to be the worst job of all.

Usually, Willie worked on the ground, feeding the tree branches into a wood chipper. But sometimes he had to go up a tree to help out one of his coworkers. One day, he tried to climb down a rope and got stuck hanging in the air with his hand caught in the rope. He almost lost a finger.

Willie was twenty feet above the ground, and there were sizzling power lines below him. To save himself, he had to cut the rope and fall to the ground. Luckily, he landed between the power lines and wasn't seriously injured.

That day, Willie quit and never went back to work for the tree-trimming company. It wasn't the right job for him—and besides, he had other plans for his life.

CHAPTER 3
Family Man

In 1950, still in search of a steady job, Willie enlisted in the US Air Force. He made it through basic training and was stationed at Lackland Air Force Base in San Antonio, Texas. He seemed to be enjoying his new military career and even dreamed about becoming a pilot. But after just nine months, he hurt his back while lifting some boxes. The doctors told him he would either have to have back surgery or leave the Air Force entirely.

Willie chose to be discharged and returned to his hometown of Abbott.

One day, he and a friend decided to stop for a cheeseburger.

There he met a sixteen-year-old waitress named Martha Jewel Matthews. She recognized Willie from seeing him play at one of the local honky-tonks. It was love at first sight—for both of them. They got married only a few months later.

Willie and Martha's life together was not always easy. Sometimes they lived with Willie's grandmother, and other times they stayed with Martha's parents. Martha continued to work as a waitress, while Willie continued to play music in bars. But they never made a lot of money.

In November 1953, Willie and Martha had their first child, a daughter they named Lana. With a baby in the house, it was more important than ever for Willie to hold down a steady job.

Baylor University

In March 1954, Willie decided to go to college at Baylor University. He hoped having a college degree would help him get a better job. He used some money he got from the Air Force to pay for school.

The Baylor campus was not very far from Willie's grandparents' house in Abbott, so Willie and Martha moved in with them temporarily. Willie was excited about going back to school. He talked about possibly becoming a lawyer when he graduated. But college was not easy for Willie.

He was always out late playing music, and that made it difficult to study. He took six different classes, including writing, math, and business. But he didn't do very well in any of them. He left Baylor after just four months.

Willie then took a job selling encyclopedias door to door. He was a good salesman, but he didn't like the idea of persuading poor families to buy expensive encyclopedia sets that they didn't need. So he quit after a few months.

Frustrated by his inability to hold down a job, Willie began drinking heavily. He and Martha started arguing a lot.

Feeling like they needed a fresh start, Willie and Martha moved to San Antonio, Texas. There Willie finally got a lucky break. He took a job as a disc jockey at a country music radio station.

All he had to do was play records and talk about the music he loved. What could be better than that?

Radio DJs

In the 1950s, entertaining announcers known as "disc jockeys" or "DJs" began popping up on radio stations across the United States. They played songs and promoted their favorite styles of music. One of the most famous DJs was Alan Freed, also known as "Moondog." He played rock and roll music, and his radio shows helped make this new music style popular. Another famous DJ was Dick Clark. He also hosted a TV show called *American Bandstand*, where he introduced many popular singers and bands to the world.

Country music had its share of famous DJs as well. One of them was Smilin' Eddie Hill, who broadcasted from the Grand Ole Opry. Another was Ralph Emery, who hosted an all-night show. People loved his soothing voice. These DJs shared the joy of country songs with their listeners and helped country music grow in popularity.

Eddie Hill

Willie got to host his own show called *Western Express*. He opened every show by singing one of his favorite songs, "Red Headed Stranger." Every time he played it, he dedicated the song to his daughter Lana. And when he came home late at night after his shift was over, he would sing the song to Lana as she fell asleep.

When he wasn't on the air, Willie used the radio station's recording equipment to record a few of his own songs. He sent this "demo" (short for *demonstration*—a sample of a song or collection of songs) out to radio stations all over Texas, hoping someone would buy one of his tunes. But he never heard back.

Willie was finally earning some decent money, enough to support his family. But he still had an itch to play and perform his own music, and he sensed that wasn't going to happen in San Antonio. So one day, he headed out on the highway, stuck out his thumb, and began a long trip halfway across the country to his next stop: Portland, Oregon.

CHAPTER 4
Struggling Musician

Willie was only six months old when his parents separated and his mother moved away. But he never forgot about her. He knew she lived in Portland, Oregon, so he decided to go see her. He also hoped he could find a better job in the bustling Northwest city.

To get to Portland, Willie had to hitchhike. But begging for rides with strangers can be very dangerous. One night, he had to sleep in a ditch on the side of the road because no one would give him a lift. Another time, he hopped onto a moving freight train. Eventually, a kindhearted truck driver helped him get to a bus station and even lent him some money to buy a bus ticket to Portland.

Willie finally made it to his mother's house in the middle of the night. Martha and baby Lana joined him there. Martha got a job as a waitress to help pay the bills while Willie looked for work as a radio DJ.

After much searching, Willie found a job at a radio station in nearby Vancouver, Washington. He resumed hosting his weekly *Western Express* country music show, which was now a three-hour program. To promote the show, he gave himself a new nickname, "Texas Willie." He also started playing his own music in bars around town. Martha gave birth to their second daughter, Susie, in early 1957.

Willie had also begun working on a new song called "Family Bible." It was inspired by Mama Nelson, who used to sing the hymn "Rock of Ages" and read from the Nelson family Bible every night after supper.

Willie was proud of his new song, which he considered his best yet.

At this time, Willie wasn't well-known enough to convince a record company to let him perform and record his own songs. He hoped to sell a song he had written to a well-known singer. As the writer, he would get paid each time the song was played on the radio. Willie was sure someone would want to buy "Family Bible," so he recorded a demo at the radio station. Now he just had to convince someone to give it a listen.

One night, while Willie was working at the radio station, a famous country singer named Mae Boren Axton stopped by to promote her latest record. After she finished her interview, Willie approached her and asked her if she would listen to his new song. Mae agreed and Willie popped his demo onto the reel-to-reel tape recorder and pressed play. Mae listened to Willie's song and smiled. She liked what she heard.

Mae Boren Axton (1914–1997)

Mae Boren Axton was born in Bardwell, Texas, and she loved music from an early age. Mae wrote songs that made people feel happy and want to dance. One of her most famous songs was "Heartbreak Hotel," a huge hit that she cowrote for Elvis Presley, a superstar in rock and roll music.

Over the course of her career, Mae wrote more than two hundred songs. Her work inspired many female performers, including Patsy Cline and Loretta Lynn. She was a legendary country music singer and songwriter who was known as the "Queen Mother of Nashville."

"Son, you have something," she said.

"I do?" Willie replied.

"You have a precious gift," Mae said. But the Pacific Northwest did not have a big country music scene. She told Willie he needed to move away from there if he was really going to succeed as a songwriter.

"To where?" Willie asked.

"Maybe back to Texas," Mae replied. "But I believe that sooner or later you're going to have to go on to Nashville"—the Tennessee city known as the country music capital of the world.

Willie couldn't afford to move to Nashville yet, so he set his sights on a return to Texas. It would take some time, though, and he and his family would make many stops along the way. They moved to Denver, Colorado, then Springfield, Missouri. Willie took odd jobs to save as much money as he could. He worked as a dishwasher, then a gas station attendant. He even went back to selling encyclopedias. At every stop along the way, Willie continued writing songs and playing them live.

Eventually, the Nelsons made it to Fort Worth, Texas, where Willie Hugh Nelson Jr., known as "Billy," was born in 1958. Willie now had a notebook filled with songs he had written. He was sure they were going to make him a star.

CHAPTER 5
A Taste of Success

From Fort Worth, Willie moved to Houston, Texas. One of Willie's first stops in Houston was a club called the Esquire Ballroom. He came there to try to sell some of his songs to established singers who were already famous so he could provide for his family.

One of the regular acts at the Esquire Ballroom was a band called the Sunset Playboys, led by a singer named Larry Butler. When he arrived at

the Esquire, Willie asked if he could talk to Larry
and play some of his songs for him. Larry agreed
to meet with Willie after the Sunset Playboys had
finished playing for the night.

Willie had a few songs he wanted to sell to
Larry, who had many popular songs on the radio
at the time. Willie sang a few of his new songs,
including "Family Bible." Larry loved them, but
he refused to buy the songs. "They're too good,"
Larry told Willie. "You need to hold onto them
for yourself."

Willie was surprised. But Larry was trying to let Willie know the value of that song over time would be much greater than the quick cash he could earn that night by selling his rights to it.

"I'm broke and I need money right now," Willie said. "I can always write some more songs." He even took Larry out to the parking lot, where Martha and the three kids were waiting in the family car. He explained that they were living in the car because they couldn't afford their own apartment. But Larry held firm.

Larry explained that, although Willie needed the money, one day he would be a big star. And Willie would want to own his songs.

Although Larry didn't buy any of Willie's songs, he wanted to help him. So he offered him a job instead. "I will put you in my band, and you can work with us. If you ever need money, I'll be here to help." Larry talked to the owner and told him that if he hired Willie for the band, Larry would pay him out of his own money.

Larry and Willie became good friends. Larry's wife, Pat, bought groceries for Willie and his family and helped them find a place to stay in Houston. He kept Willie in his band until Willie had saved up enough money to move to Nashville.

Larry had his own radio show in Houston, and he gave Willie a job at the radio station as a DJ. Willie used his time on the air to promote his shows with the Sunset Playboys.

Willie enjoyed playing live and being in a band, but he still believed he could become successful as a professional songwriter. He wanted to earn enough to support his family. After not selling a single song to Larry Butler, he tried again with another Houston musician named Paul Buskirk.

Paul Buskirk

Paul owned a music store and hired Willie to give guitar lessons in the back of the store. The two men became friends. One evening, they were having dinner together. As usual, Willie didn't have enough money to pay for his meal. Instead, he sang his song "Family Bible" to Paul and offered to sell it to him for fifty dollars plus the price of their dinner. Paul was eager to help his friend, so he bought the song. He liked another of Willie's new tunes, "Night Life," even more, and agreed to give him $150 for that one. Willie had finally made his first professional song sales.

The $200 came in handy, but it was a tiny amount compared to what Willie would make if one of his songs became a hit. In December 1959, Paul Buskirk asked a singer named Claude Gray to record "Family Bible." When the song was released, it became very popular and reached number seven on the country music chart. Because of the success of "Family Bible," Willie Nelson became well-known as a songwriter in Houston. More importantly, he now had enough money to move to Nashville, where he believed all his dreams of fame and fortune would come true.

Claude Gray

Music City, USA

The city of Nashville, Tennessee, is known as Music City, USA, because of its long history as a center for the music industry—especially American country music. People from all around the world come to Nashville to write, record, and listen to music. Many hope to become famous musicians and singers. Nashville even has a street called Music Row, home to many music studios and record companies.

The Grand Ole Opry, a popular country music radio show, has been broadcast out of Nashville since 1925. Many famous singers, like Dolly Parton and Johnny Cash, have sung on the program. Although country music is the most famous style in Nashville, today people play and record rock, pop, and many other types of music there, too. Music City, USA, is a place where music is created and celebrated by everyone.

Music Row, Nashville, Tennessee

CHAPTER 6
The Hitmaker

Willie had finally made it to Nashville, but he did not arrive in style. In fact, his beat-up old car conked out on the way into town. He had to leave it by the side of the road.

And even more hard times awaited him in Music City. Although he had sold his first few songs in Texas, no one in Tennessee knew who he was. None of the Nashville record companies wanted to meet with him. So Willie spent most of his days drinking in a bar called Tootsie's, where all of the city's struggling musicians hung out. Willie tried selling his songs to anyone who'd listen, but nobody was buying.

One day, Willie was having trouble trying to think of a new song. He stared at the walls, searching for inspiration. Then he got an idea. "Hello, walls," he sang. Suddenly, the words to a song flowed out of him. It was about a lonely man sitting by himself in an empty house, talking to empty walls.

Tootsie's

Willie played "Hello Walls" for his musician friends, hoping one of them would want to record it. But no one would buy it. They thought it was too silly and funny, and that people wouldn't understand the serious message in the song. Willie was disappointed, so he went down to Tootsie's. There he ran into a friend of his, a country singer named Faron Young. Willie played "Hello Walls" for Faron and offered to sell him the song for $400. Faron refused, but he promised to record it later. Willie said he needed the money right now, so Faron agreed to loan Willie the $400 if he promised not to sell the song to anyone else.

A short time later, Faron was ready to record "Hello Walls." He sang the song in a smooth voice that made it sound more like he was talking. His style made the song seem personal, as if Faron was having a conversation with the listener. The song that nobody wanted went on to become one of the biggest hits of 1961.

When "Hello Walls" had been played on the radio enough times, Willie received a big check for his share of the profits. He was so happy that he repaid Faron Young his $400 loan—in cash. "You don't owe me anything," Faron said. "If anyone owes anyone here, it's me who owes you." The "silly" little song had helped make Faron Young a star.

After "Hello Walls" became a hit, Willie felt like he was on a winning streak with his songwriting. He had a new tune called "Crazy" that he thought might be a good fit for country music star Patsy Cline. But after getting turned down so many times, Willie was afraid to approach Patsy directly. When Patsy's husband, Charlie Dick, heard the song, he agreed that it would be perfect for Patsy and convinced her to record it. Patsy's rendition of "Crazy" became a huge hit—one of the most popular songs ever played on jukeboxes.

Willie used the money he earned from "Crazy" to buy a new Cadillac car for his wife Martha. But while Willie was finally starting to gain success as a songwriter, his home life wasn't going so well. He was always working and hardly ever at home. This made Martha very sad, and she and Willie started having more frequent fights. Eventually, they agreed to get a divorce. Martha took their three kids and moved to Las Vegas.

In 1963, Willie married a woman named Shirley Collie. They bought a farmhouse in a town called Ridgetop, near Nashville. A short time later, Willie's children from his marriage to Martha left Las Vegas and came to live with Willie and Shirley on the farm.

Willie and Shirley at home in Ridgetop

Willie was ready to take the next step in his career. Now that he was an established songwriter, he wanted to start recording his own songs and full  albums. In 1964, Willie signed a contract with the record label RCA Victor to release his first album of all original songs, *Country Willie: His Own Songs*.

That same year, Willie was asked to perform at the Grand Ole Opry, the most famous showcase in country music. This was a big deal and showed that people were starting to recognize him as a singer and not just a songwriter.

The Grand Ole Opry

The Grand Ole Opry is a popular music radio show that began in 1925 and continues to this day. Broadcast each week out of Nashville, the Opry provides a showcase for performers in country, bluegrass, folk, and gospel music, as

well as comedy skits. Millions of people around the world listen to the show on the radio or internet. Thousands more visit Nashville to attend a live taping. Many famous country music stars have been featured on the show, including Hank Williams, Patsy Cline, Johnny Cash, and Dolly Parton.

Stage of the original Grand Ole Opry

Patsy Cline (1932–1963)

Patsy Cline was born in Winchester, Virginia. She loved singing from a young age in school and church. Everyone could tell that her voice was special.

When Patsy grew up, she started singing live on the radio, and then making music in the recording studio. Her biggest hits were "Crazy" and "I Fall to Pieces." People all over the world loved her music. Sadly, Patsy's life was cut short. She died in a plane crash when she was only thirty. But her music lives on, and she is still considered one of the most beloved singers in country music.

CHAPTER 7
New Beginnings

In the late 1960s, Willie wrote and recorded a string of hit songs and albums. But an unfortunate accident almost derailed his songwriting career. At a concert in 1969, someone accidentally stepped on Willie's guitar and broke it. Willie took the broken guitar to a repairman who tried to fix it, but it was too damaged.

Instead, the repairman offered to sell Willie a brand-new guitar called the Martin N-20. Willie loved the sound the instrument made and agreed to buy it for $750. In fact, Willie loved his new guitar so much he decided it had to have its own pet name. But what to call it? Willie thought about it and came up with the name "Trigger" after the name of the horse ridden by singing cowboy

Roy Rogers. "I figured this is my horse!" Willie declared. Trigger the guitar became one of Willie's prized possessions.

Willie was once again spending time touring and promoting his music. While he was on the road, Willie had begun seeing another woman,

Connie Koepke. In October 1969, she gave birth to a baby girl they named Paula. When Shirley found out that Willie had had a child with another woman, she sued him for divorce and moved out of their house. Connie and baby Paula moved in. She and Willie were married a short time later. But Willie's new home life wouldn't last long.

Shortly before Christmas in 1970, Willie was in Nashville when he got a phone call. His house was on fire! In a panic, Willie raced back home to find his house in flames. Luckily, Connie, the baby, and his other children had escaped unharmed. But Willie feared that he would lose all his belongings in the blaze. Though the firefighters warned him it was unsafe, Willie charged into the burning house and saved his new guitar, Trigger, from the inferno. Everything else he owned was destroyed.

Willie decided that the fire was a sign from God that he needed to change the way he was living. With no house left in Nashville, he and Connie moved to a place near Austin, Texas. Willie announced that he was taking a break from recording new music. Instead, he spent his days reading the Bible, smoking marijuana, and thinking about what he wanted to do next. Marijuana is a plant that Willie claimed help him achieve the relaxed frame of mind he needed during this period of reflection. At the time, however, it was illegal.

After some months away, Willie decided to return to recording music. He signed a new record deal and started releasing songs and albums again. Some of Willie's biggest hits and most beloved tunes, like "Shotgun Willie" and "Red Headed Stranger"—

the song he once played on the radio before his DJ sets—were recorded during this period.

While playing live shows to promote these new records, Willie noticed a lot of new faces in the crowds. Younger fans, many of them teenagers, were starting to attend his concerts. In the early 1970s, many boys and young men were starting to wear their hair long and growing long beards.

They were known as "hippies," and many had never been fans of traditional country music. But they loved the type of music Willie was playing.

Inspired by his fans, Willie began to grow his own hair out. Sometimes he pulled it back into a ponytail or tied it into two braids. He stopped trimming his beard and stopped wearing suits and ties. Instead he wore jeans with "bell-bottom" flares and tied a red bandanna around his  forehead. The Willie Nelson look was born.

In the summer of 1973, Willie decided to put on a special show for his new fans. He called it his Fourth of July Picnic. Willie invited some of his best friends to a ranch in Dripping Springs, Texas,

to play the concert with him, including Rita Coolidge, Waylon Jennings, Kris Kristofferson, and John Prine. The Fourth of July Picnic was a huge success, attracting more than 40,000 fans.

Fourth of July Picnic, 1973

For many of them, it was the first country music concert they had ever attended. Willie decided to make it an annual event.

Two days after the first Picnic concert, Willie's wife Connie gave birth to their second child together, a daughter named Amy Lee. Now that his family life had settled down, Willie was riding high as a singer and songwriter. His concerts were selling out and his songs were getting played constantly on the radio.

In October 1975, Willie's recording of an old  country song, "Blue Eyes Crying in the Rain," became his first number one hit as a singer. It ended the year as the third best-selling country song of 1975. At the following Grammy Awards, Willie collected the award for Best Country Vocal Performance, Male. It was the first of twelve Grammy Awards Willie has collected so far over the course of his career.

Critics loved Willie's new albums as well. They even came up with a special term, "outlaw country," to describe the style of music that Willie, Waylon Jennings, and Kris Kristofferson had made so popular.

Willie's Fourth of July Picnic became a Texas tradition. In 1974, the picnic was expanded to a three-day festival. In 1975, the picnic moved to Liberty Hill, Texas, and attracted 90,000 fans—more than double the number of people who attended the first event two years before. The state of Texas declared the Fourth "Willie Nelson Day" in his honor. It was a good time to be Willie Nelson—and it was about to get even better.

CHAPTER 8
Willie Nelson, Superstar

By the late 1970s, Willie Nelson was one of the  most famous country singers in America. His 1978 album *Waylon & Willie*, recorded with his friend Waylon Jennings, was a huge hit and established the new style of music called "outlaw country." Willie even had a fan in the White House. President Jimmy Carter, who took office in 1977, was a huge supporter of country music. In 1979, Willie gave the president an award for helping to promote country artists like him.

To return the favor, President Carter invited Willie to perform at the White House. In September 1980, Willie, Connie, and their two daughters arrived in Washington, DC, for a two-day visit. Willie and the president jogged and went swimming together in the morning. Then at night Willie put on a show on the White House lawn. Willie and the First Lady, Rosalynn Carter, even performed a duet together.

The First Lady had no trouble with the lyrics since both she and her husband knew many of Willie's songs by heart.

As Willie's fame grew, he started to think about branching out beyond music. When director Sydney Pollack offered Willie a role in his new movie *The Electric Horseman*, Willie jumped at the chance to act. Willie found that he liked acting and looked for a chance to star in a movie of his own.

The Electric Horseman, 1979

In 1980, Willie got his chance. In his second film, *Honeysuckle Rose*, Willie played the part of Buck Bonham, a struggling country singer who travels around the country in a beat-up tour bus. The producers asked Willie to write a theme song for the  movie. The song he came up with, "On the Road Again," turned out to be one of Willie's biggest hits. It was even nominated for an Academy Award—called an Oscar—for Best Original Song. In "On the Road Again," Willie sings about the joys of life as a traveling musician, "going places that I've never been," alongside the members of a band:

The life I love is making music with my friends
I can't wait to get on the road again.

Willie was now a very wealthy man. He used some of the money he made to buy his own golf course near Austin, Texas. Always fascinated by martial arts, he started training in tae kwon do and was able to become a black belt in that fighting style.

Willie continued to release hit records throughout the 1980s, including now-classic songs like "To All the Girls I've Loved Before," with Spanish singer Julio Iglesias, and "Always on My Mind." He formed the country supergroup the Highwaymen with Waylon Jennings, Kris Kristofferson, and Johnny Cash. But there were setbacks as well. Both of Willie's parents passed away, as did his beloved grandmother, Mama Nelson.

In 1985, Willie was invited to join the other superstars of popular music in a project called USA for Africa. Celebrities were coming together to help raise awareness about world hunger. They recorded the song "We Are the World," written by Michael Jackson and Lionel Richie, to raise money for the starving people of Ethiopia. The song was performed by a supergroup that included Stevie Wonder, Paul Simon, Tina Turner, Diana Ross, Dionne Warwick, Bruce Springsteen, and others.

The Highwaymen

The Highwaymen were a country music supergroup formed in 1985 by Willie Nelson, Johnny Cash, Waylon Jennings, and Kris Kristofferson. Each member was already a very famous solo artist who brought his own unique style to the group. The Highwaymen helped popularize the outlaw country movement, blending traditional country with rock influences. Their first album, *Highwayman*, became a huge hit, topping the country charts and earning critical acclaim. With hit songs like "Highwayman" and "Desperados Waiting for a Train," the Highwaymen created a lasting legacy that influenced generations of musicians.

Inspired by USA for Africa's success, Willie decided it was time to do something about an important cause closer to home: America's struggling family farmers.

Willie and some of his friends in the music business, including Bob Dylan, Johnny Cash, Neil Young, and John Cougar Mellencamp, got together to help organize a benefit concert called Farm Aid. The first Farm Aid concert took place on September 22, 1985, at Memorial Stadium in Champaign, Illinois. The concert was a huge success and raised $7 million for family farmers across America. And in 1987, Willie traveled to Washington, DC, to testify before a United States Senate committee about the plight of family farmers.

In 1988, Willie's marriage to Connie ended in divorce. Willie kept busy with new projects, including a TV movie called *Stagecoach* starring the other members of his Highwaymen supergroup.

Farm Aid, 1985

While they were filming, Willie met the movie's makeup artist, Ann Marie D'Angelo, known as Annie. They hit it off instantly and soon began dating. Five years later, they were married. Together they had two sons, Lukas Autry and Jacob Micah.

Willie and Annie

As the 1990s dawned, Willie looked forward to a fresh start with his new wife and continued success in show business. But there were sad times ahead as well.

CHAPTER 9
Living Legend

In 1991, Willie and Annie decided to move to Hawaii. They already owned a house there, and were spending more time there with their two young sons. They loved the natural beauty of Hawaii. And they had grown tired of shooing away Willie's fans, who would often turn up at the front door of his home in Texas, looking for autographs.

Willie was just starting to enjoy his new, more private life on the beach when tragedy struck. His son Willie Jr. died. Willie was very upset and began to spend even more time by himself in his new home. For a man who loved being on the road and "making music with his friends," this was a sad and lonely time.

Things got even worse when the US government's Internal Revenue Service (IRS) discovered that Willie had not been filing his taxes properly. He owed the government a lot more money than he and his manager had claimed. The IRS brought a lawsuit against Willie, seeking millions of dollars in unpaid taxes.

To help pay off his tax bill, Willie had to go back on the road. Throughout the 1990s, he toured constantly. He also recorded several new albums.

Willie Nelson's tour bus

But he could never seem to scrape together enough to pay the entire amount that he owed.

Finally, Willie struck a deal with the IRS. He agreed to put out a "Greatest Hits" album and let the government have all the profits. The record was called *The IRS Tapes: Who'll Buy My Memories?* and while it didn't cover all of Willie's tax bill, he was able to greatly reduce the amount 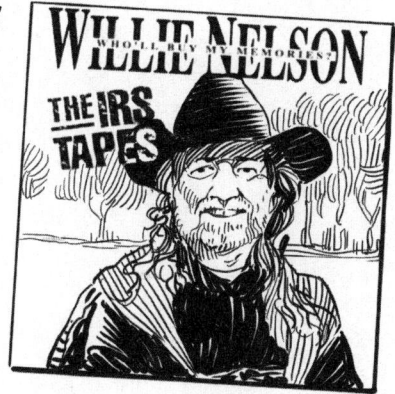 he owed. Eventually, the IRS agreed to drop its lawsuit.

While these were tough times for Willie, he was still able to enjoy the admiration of his fans and friends in the music industry. In 1993, Willie was inducted into the Country Music Hall of Fame. In 1998, he was honored by the Kennedy Center with a lifetime achievement award.

Willie Nelson at the Kennedy Center Honors, 1998

In 2003, he celebrated his seventieth birthday with a television special on the USA Network. And Bob Dylan, Snoop Dogg, and Paul Simon were just some of the artists who joined him to record new music together over the years.

During this time, Willie also dedicated himself to improving his physical fitness through one of his favorite childhood pursuits: martial arts. After twenty years of training, Willie earned his fifth-degree black belt in a Korean martial art called GongKwon Yusul. He strapped on his new belt in a ceremony held in Austin, Texas.

While martial arts kept his body in shape, marijuana continued to help Willie mellow his mind. In the 2000s, attitudes began changing about recreational use of the drug. Many US states moved toward making marijuana legal for adults over twenty-one. At his concerts, Willie spoke out strongly in favor of the legalization of marijuana. He even started his own marijuana business called Willie's Reserve. Another company, Willie's Remedy, was aimed at medical users. Both were very successful.

In addition to Farm Aid, there were other charitable causes that took up Willie's time. When the coronavirus pandemic hit the United States in March 2020, Willie organized a series of virtual benefit concerts that raised close to a million dollars for people suffering from the effects of COVID-19 lockdowns.

Many people slow down as they get older, but Willie Nelson only seemed to pick up speed.

The year 2023 proved to be full of milestones for Willie, who released two new studio albums and continued to tour the country with his band. In February, Willie took home two Grammys at the 65th Annual Grammy Awards, including Best Country Album for *A Beautiful Time*. Throughout the course of his career, Willie has earned a total of twelve Grammy Awards, as well as their Lifetime Achievement Award.

In late April, Willie celebrated his ninetieth birthday with an all-star concert spanning two days at the famous Hollywood Bowl in Los Angeles. The epic birthday party concert included Keith Richards, Snoop Dogg, Sheryl Crow, George Strait, and Neil Young. At the end of the show, Willie's sons Lukas and Micah came onstage to welcome their dad. For the grand finale, all the performers joined together to sing a medley of gospel songs.

"Happy birthday to me!" Willie proclaimed, prompting the entire audience to join him in a chorus of "Happy Birthday."

Willie onstage with Keith Richards

But the year of celebrations wasn't quite over.

On October 31, Willie released a new book, *Energy Follows Thought: The Stories Behind My Songs*. In it, he told the stories behind the lyrics of some of his favorite songs. And on November 3, Willie was inducted into the Rock and Roll Hall of Fame.

Willie Nelson is a rare country songwriter and musician who is beloved by fans of rock, pop, and hip-hop. His movies and TV specials have helped him reach an even wider audience. And his charitable work for causes like famine relief and family farms has earned him the respect of activists around the world. He has lived a long and sometimes troubled life with its share of challenges. And Willie would be the first person to admit that he is far from perfect. But his one-of-a-kind style and "outlaw" attitude have made him one of America's most beloved entertainers across two centuries.

From humble beginnings, he grew to become one of the most successful recording artists of all time. Few people can match his talent for writing hit songs, and his live shows are always popular. One thing is for sure: There will never be another Willie Nelson.

Timeline of Willie Nelson's Life

1933	Willie Nelson is born in Abbott, Texas
1947	Begins playing in the band Bud Fletcher and the Texans
1950	Graduates from high school and joins the US Air Force
1952	Marries Martha Matthews
1960	Moves to Nashville
1961	Song "Crazy" becomes a top ten country single
1963	Marries Shirley Collie
1969	Buys a Martin guitar that he nicknames Trigger
1971	Marries Connie Koepke
1973	First Fourth of July Picnic concert
1975	Has his first number one country hit with album single "Blue Eyes Crying in the Rain"
1980	Records the hit song "On the Road Again"
1985	Supergroup album *Highwayman* reaches the top twenty
	Organizes the first Farm Aid concert
1991	Marries Annie D'Angelo
1993	Inducted into the Country Music Hall of Fame
1998	Receives Kennedy Center Honors lifetime achievement award
2023	Celebrates his ninetieth birthday at the Hollywood Bowl
	Inducted into the Rock and Roll Hall of Fame

Timeline of the World

1933 — Franklin D. Roosevelt is inaugurated as the thirty-second US president

1952 — Puerto Rico becomes a US commonwealth

1955 — Cellist Yo-Yo Ma is born in France

1963 — President John F. Kennedy is assassinated in Dallas by Lee Harvey Oswald

1969 — Astronaut Neil Armstrong becomes the first person to walk on the moon

1970 — Pop group the Beatles breaks up

1981 — MTV, a cable TV music video channel, premieres

1996 — Atlanta, Georgia, hosts the Summer Olympic Games

2001 — Terrorist attacks kill almost three thousand people in New York, Pennsylvania, and Washington, DC, on September 11

2008 — Barack Obama is elected the first Black president of the United States

2010 — Deepwater Horizon oil rig explodes, causing the largest marine oil spill in history

2020 — COVID-19 pandemic begins

2023 — Charles III is crowned king of the United Kingdom of Great Britain and Northern Ireland

Bibliography

Nelson, Willie. *It's a Long Story: My Life*. With David Ritz.
New York: Little, Brown and Company, 2015.

Nelson, Willie. *Roll Me Up and Smoke Me When I Die: Musings from the Road*. New York: William Morrow, 2012.

Nelson, Willie. *The Tao of Willie: A Guide to the Happiness in Your Heart*. With Turk Pipkin. New York: Gotham, 2006.

Nelson, Willie. *Willie: An Autobiography*. With Bud Shrake.
New York: Simon & Schuster, 1988.

Nelson, Willie, and Bobbie Nelson. *Me and Sister Bobbie: True Tales from the Family Band*. New York: Random House, 2020.

Vaughan, Andrew. *Willie Nelson: American Icon*. New York: Union Square & Co, 2017.